J

ALL AROUND THE WORLD
DENMARK

by Kristine Spanier, MLIS

pogo

Ideas for Parents and Teachers

Pogo Books let children practice reading informational text while introducing them to nonfiction features such as headings, labels, sidebars, maps, and diagrams, as well as a table of contents, glossary, and index.

Carefully leveled text with a strong photo match offers early fluent readers the support they need to succeed.

Before Reading

- "Walk" through the book and point out the various nonfiction features. Ask the student what purpose each feature serves.
- Look at the glossary together. Read and discuss the words.

Read the Book

- Have the child read the book independently.
- Invite him or her to list questions that arise from reading.

After Reading

- Discuss the child's questions. Talk about how he or she might find answers to those questions.
- Prompt the child to think more. Ask: The people of Denmark work hard to protect the environment. What do you do to protect the environment?

Pogo Books are published by Jump!
5357 Penn Avenue South
Minneapolis, MN 55419
www.jumplibrary.com

Library of Congress Cataloging-in-Publication Data

Names: Spanier, Kristine, author.
Title: Denmark / by Kristine Spanier.
Description: Minneapolis, MN: Pogo Books, 2021.
Series: All around the world | Includes index.
Audience: Ages 7–10 | Audience: Grades 2–3
Identifiers: LCCN 2019039879 (print)
LCCN 2019039880 (ebook)
ISBN 9781645273325 (hardcover)
ISBN 9781645273332 (paperback)
ISBN 9781645273349 (ebook)
Subjects: LCSH: Denmark–Juvenile literature.
Classification: LCC DL109 .S73 2021 (print)
LCC DL109 (ebook) | DDC 948.9–dc23
LC record available at https://lccn.loc.gov/2019039879
LC ebook record available at https://lccn.loc.gov/2019039880

Editor: Jenna Gleisner
Designer: Molly Ballanger

Photo Credits: SuppalakKlabdee/iStock, cover; miroslav_1/iStock, 1; Pixfiction/Shutterstock, 3; Alexander A. Trofimov/Shutterstock, 4; Dreamer Company/Shutterstock, 5; mauritius images GmbH/Alamy, 6-7; icarmen13/iStock, 8-9; Paii VeGa/Shutterstock, 10; Vrezh Gyozalyan/Shutterstock, 11; BreakingTheWalls/iStock, 12-13tl; Jezperklauzen/iStock, 12-13tr; Coatesy/Shutterstock, 12-13bl; Mats B/Shutterstock, 12-13br; Pocholo Calapre/Shutterstock, 14; miroslav110/Shutterstock, 15; Food Via Lenses/Shutterstock, 16-17; Thomas Tolstrup/Getty, 18-19; Ingus Kruklitis/Shutterstock, 20-21; ustun ibisoglu/Shutterstock, 23.

Printed in the United States of America at Corporate Graphics in North Mankato, Minnesota.

TABLE OF CONTENTS

CHAPTER 1

WELCOME TO DENMARK!

Hej! This is how you say hello in Denmark. Kronborg Castle sits near the Baltic Sea. It was once a **symbol** of Denmark's power.

Kronborg Castle

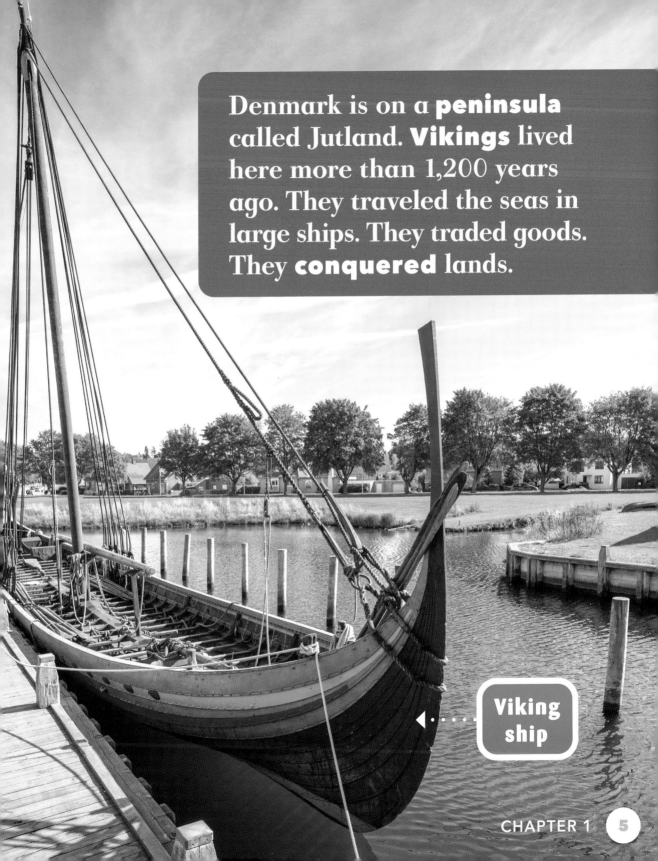

Denmark is on a **peninsula** called Jutland. **Vikings** lived here more than 1,200 years ago. They traveled the seas in large ships. They traded goods. They **conquered** lands.

Viking ship

More than 400 islands are here. The Great Belt Bridge links the islands of Zealand and Funen. The Øresund Bridge connects Denmark and Sweden. Cars and trucks travel on the top **deck**. A train track is on the lower deck. It turns into a tunnel. It goes under the sea!

DID YOU KNOW?

People in Denmark are never more than 32 miles (52 kilometers) from the sea.

Øresund Bridge

tunnel

Greenland

The Faroe Islands are a **territory** of Denmark. So is Greenland. It is the world's largest island. More than 80 percent of it is covered in ice! Its **citizens** are considered Danish.

CHAPTER 2

LAND AND ANIMALS

Denmark's land is flat. The highest point is only 568 feet (173 meters)! Most of the land is good for farming. Wheat and barley grow here. Wind farms are here, too. **Wind turbines** are **exports**.

wind turbine

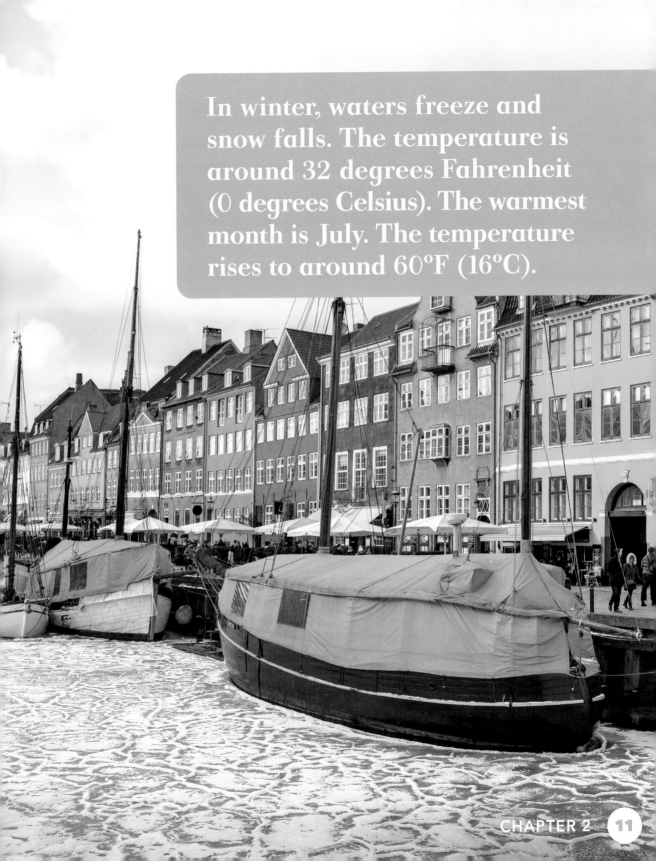

In winter, waters freeze and snow falls. The temperature is around 32 degrees Fahrenheit (0 degrees Celsius). The warmest month is July. The temperature rises to around 60°F (16°C).

flatfish

cod

hedgehog

red deer

The seas near Denmark are filled with fish. Flatfish, cod, and herring are just a few. Animals roam the land. You might spot a hedgehog or a red deer!

CHAPTER 3
LIFE IN DENMARK

Copenhagen is the **capital**. A **statue** is here. It is called The Little Mermaid. It is based on the fairy tale. It is a symbol of the city.

The Little Mermaid

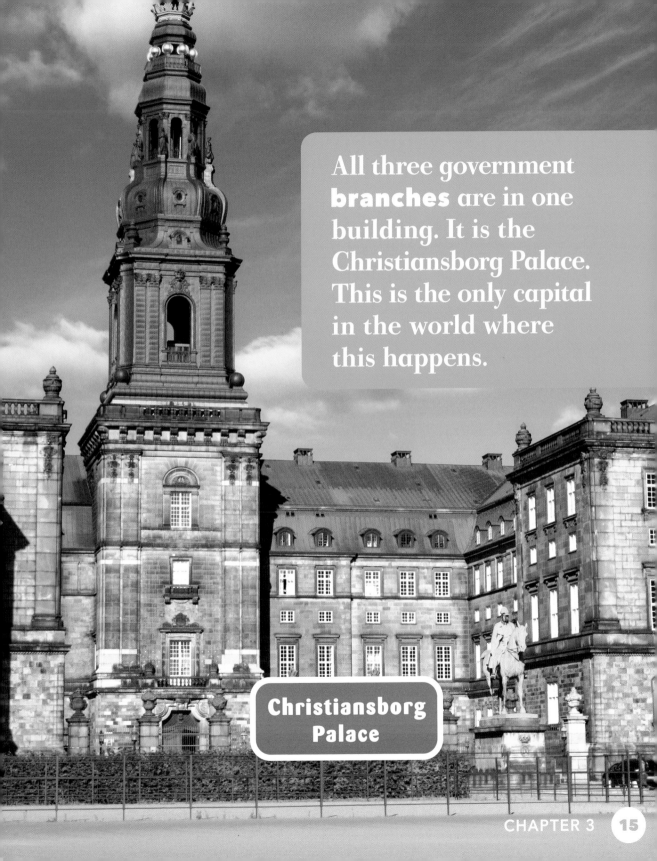

All three government **branches** are in one building. It is the Christiansborg Palace. This is the only capital in the world where this happens.

Christiansborg Palace

What is for dinner? Many families eat meatballs or hamburgers with gravy. Potatoes and pickled red beets are good side dishes. Sweet waffles with ice cream are a tasty dessert. So is licorice!

Smørrebrød ·····▶

TAKE A LOOK!

Smørrebrød is for lunch. It is eaten with a fork and knife. Rye bread with butter is at the bottom. The top is piled with favorite ingredients. What would you choose?

onion slices

cucumber slices

parsley

dill

cheese

hard-boiled eggs

pickled herring

meatballs

salami

ham

roast beef

rye bread

Some children go to preschool or kindergarten. Others start school when they are seven years old. They go until they are 16. Some students begin to work after ninth grade. Others might learn a **trade** or go to college.

WHAT DO YOU THINK?

Many kids here bike to school. The flat land makes it easy to get around on bikes. How do you travel where you live? Do you bike?

Tivoli Gardens is one of the oldest amusement parks in the world. It opened in 1843.

What else do people do for fun? People in Denmark like to swim, sail, and row. Soccer is the most popular sport. Badminton is fun, too.

What would you like to do in Denmark?

WHAT DO YOU THINK?

Many activities here involve water. Why do you think this is? What kind of activities or sports are popular where you live? Why?

Tivoli
Gardens

QUICK FACTS & TOOLS

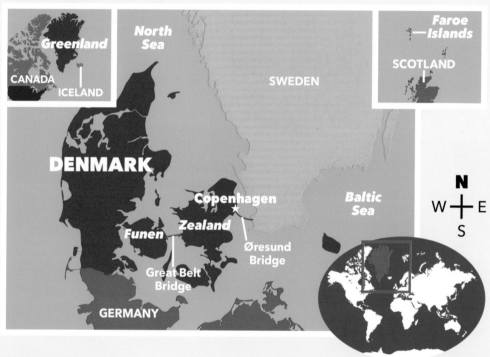

DENMARK

Location: Northern Europe

Size: 16,639 square miles (43,095 square kilometers)

Population: 5,809,502 (July 2018 estimate)

Capital: Copenhagen

Type of Government: parliamentary constitutional monarchy

Languages: Danish, English, Faroese, Greenlandic

Exports: wind turbines, instruments, meat and dairy products, fish, furniture

Currency: Danish krone

branches: The divisions of an organization, such as the government.

capital: A city where government leaders meet.

citizens: People who have full rights in a certain country, such as the right to work and the right to vote.

conquered: Defeated and took control of an enemy or territory.

deck: A floor or platform.

exports: Products sold to different countries.

peninsula: A piece of land that sticks out from a larger landmass and is almost completely surrounded by water.

statue: A sculpture, model, or cast that represents something or someone.

symbol: An object or design that stands for, suggests, or represents something else.

territory: Land under the control of a state, nation, or ruler.

trade: A particular job, especially one that requires working with one's hands or machines.

Vikings: Scandinavian people who invaded the coasts of Europe and explored the North American coast between the 700s and 1000s.

wind turbines: Large devices with blades that are rotated by the wind to generate electricity.

Denmark's currency

INDEX

TO LEARN MORE

Finding more information is as easy as 1, 2, 3.

1. Go to www.factsurfer.com
2. Enter "Denmark" into the search box.
3. Click the "Surf" button to see a list of websites.

FACT SURFER